Other books by Exley:
Golf a Celebration
Golf Jokes
Golf Quotations
The Fanatics Guide to Golf
The Crazy World of Golf
The World's Greatest Golf Cartoons
Golf Score Book

Published simultaneously in 1994 by Exley
Publications in Great Britain, and Exley Giftbooks in
the USA.

ISBN 1-85015-521-6

Pictures selected by Helen Exley.
Designed by The Pinpoint Design Company.
Picture research by P. A. Goldberg and J. Clift/Image
Select, London.
Typesetting by Delta, Watford.
Printed and bound in Hungary.

**Exley Publications Ltd, 16 Chalk Hill, Watford,
Herts WD1 4BN, UK.
Exley Giftbooks, 232 Madison Avenue, Suite 1206,
New York, NY 10016, USA.**

Cover: *MIKE VAUGHN*
The Image Bank

Title page: GOLF TOURNAMENT
TOM MCNEELY
The Image Bank

• *The Love of* •
GOLF
A D D R E S S B O O K

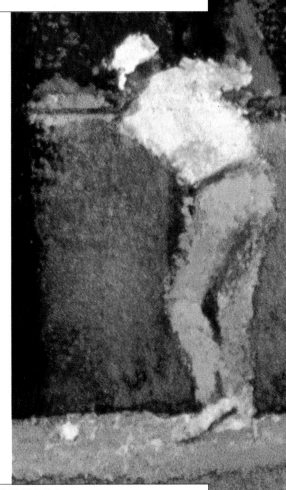

EXLEY
NEW YORK • WATFORD, UK

A

---

*Golf is like a love affair: If you don't take it
seriously, it's not fun; if you do take it seriously,
it breaks your heart.*
ARNOLD DALY

B

GOLF SHOT OUT OF SAND
TODD DONEY
The Image Bank

B

_____

_____

_____

_____

_____

_____

Golf puts a man's character on the anvil and his richest qualities - patience, poise, restraint - to the flame.
BILLY CASPER

B

C

I couldn't wait for the sun to come up the next morning so that I could get out on the course again.
BEN HOGAN

C

GOLFER IN TOURNAMENT PUTTING ON GREEN
CHUCK HAMRICK
The Image Bank

C

*It means...getting close to nature, fresh air
and exercise, a sweeping of mental cobwebs and
a genuine relaxation of tired tissues.*
DAVID FORGAN

D

It is a test of temper, a trial of honour,
a revealer of character.
DAVID FORGAN

MAN GOLFING IN TOURNAMENT
LISA POMERANTZ
The Image Bank
Opposite: GOLFER "DRIVING" OUT OF SAND BUNKER
FRANCIS LABARTHE
The Image Bank

D

BEN HOGAN TAKES BRITISH OPEN 1953
BILL BRAUER, Sarah Fabian Baddiel
Opposite: 1960 US OPEN ARNOLD PALMER'S FIRST
"CHARGE", *BILL BRAUER*
Sarah Fabian Baddiel

... golf has never had a truly great player who was not also a person of extraordinary character.
FRANK D. "SANDY" TUTAM, JR.

F

GREGORY ALEXANDER
through Montague Ward, Wadhurst

F

_____

_____

_____

_____

_____

_____

*I don't say my golf game is bad; but if I grew
tomatoes, they'd come up sliced.*
MILLER BARBER

G

GOLFERS ON THE GREEN BY OCEAN
GARY MCLAUGHLIN
The Image Bank

G

Willis' Rule of Golf:
You can't lose an old golf ball.
JOHN WILLIS

H

CARLOS LENCINAS
The Image Bank

H

Like life, golf can be humbling. However, little good
comes from brooding about mistakes we've made.
The next shot, in golf or in life, is the big one.
GRANTLAND RICE

I J

There is a right or wrong way of hitting
a yard putt. The right way is bliss,
the wrong purgatory.
DAVID FORGAN

TWO GOLFERS ON GREEN PUTTING
BILL FARNSWORTH
The Image Bank
Opposite: GOLFING
RUSTY JONES
The Image Bank

J

US OPEN PLAY-OFF 1962 NICKLAUS 71, PALMER 74
BILL BRAUER
Sarah Fabian Baddiel

_____

_____

_____

_____

_____

_____

*There is one thing in this world that is dumber
than playing golf. That is watching someone
else play golf....*
PETER ANDREWS

_____

_____

_____

_____

_____

_____

Hope: "Okay, what's wrong with my game?"
Palmer: "If you're talking about golf, that's not
your game."
ARNOLD PALMER, B. 1929 AND BOB HOPE, B.1904

M

GOLF TROPHY PRESENTATION
CHUCK HAMRICK
The Image Bank

M

_____

_____

_____

_____

_____

_____

The more I practise, the luckier, I get.
GARY PLAYER. B.1935

M

SNEAD AND HOGAN PLAY-OFF 1954 MASTERS
BILL BRAUER
© *Sarah Fabian Baddiel*
.Opposite: THE BEST WAY TO DRIVE
© *Sarah Fabian Baddiel*

N

_____

_____

_____

_____

_____

_____

Golf appeals to the idiot in us and the child....
Just how childlike golf players become is proven
by their frequent inability to count past five.
JOHN UPDIKE, B.1932

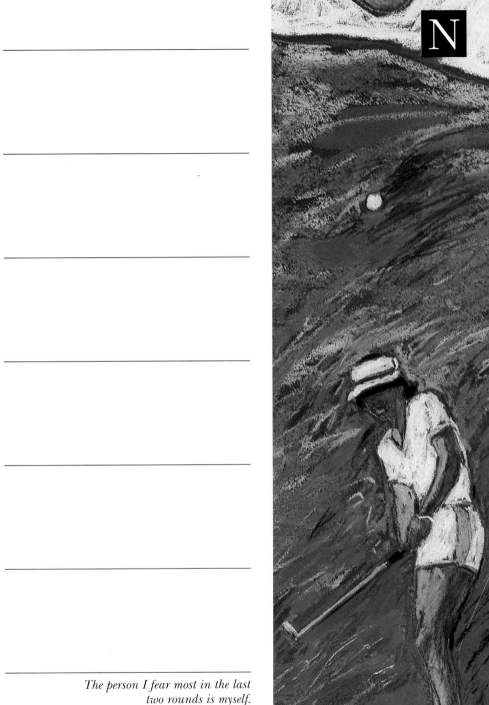

_____

_____

_____

_____

_____

_____

_____

The person I fear most in the last
two rounds is myself.
TOM WATSON, B.1949

FRANÇOIS DARDELET, *The Image Bank*

GERALD ROLAND TUDER
Sarah Fabian Baddiel

_____

_____

_____

_____

_____

_____

*Never break your putter and your driver in the
same round or you're dead.*
TOMMY BOLT

P

I say this without any reservations whatsoever: It is impossible to outplay an opponent you can't outthink.
LAWSON LITTLE

_____

_____

_____

_____

_____

_____

Golf does strange things.... It makes liars out of
honest men, cheats out of altruists, cowards out
of brave men and fools out of everybody.
                                        MILTON GROSS

R

GOLFER DRIVING BALL OUT OF SAND TRAP
BONNOT
The Image Bank

R

Competitive golf is played mainly on a five-and-a-half inch course, the space between your ears.
BOBBY JONES

R

FRANCIS OUIMET WINS THE US OPEN 1913
BILL BRAUER
Sarah Fabian Baddiel

S

_____

_____

_____

_____

_____

_____

The mind messes up more shots than the body.
TOMMY BOLT

S

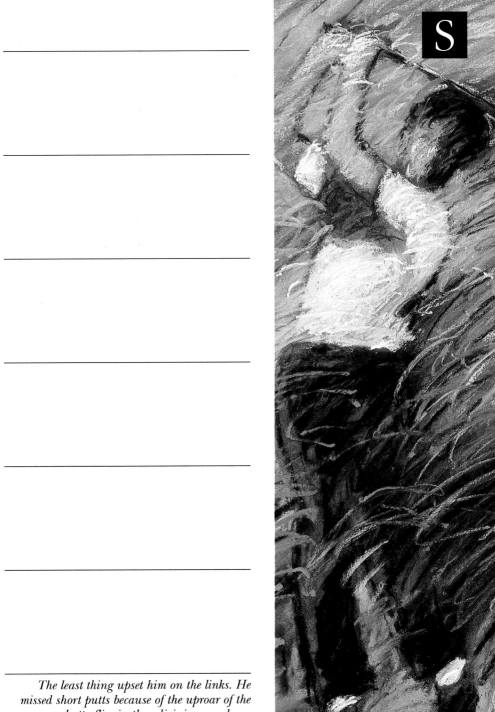

S

The least thing upset him on the links. He missed short putts because of the uproar of the butterflies in the adjoining meadows.
P.G. WODEHOUSE (1881-1975)

S

S

_Never hurry, never worry and always remember
to smell the flowers along the way._
WALTER HAGEN (1892-1969)

CARLOS LENCINAS, _The Image Bank_

T

THE FIFTH TEE, ST. ANDREWS, 1921
JOHN SUTTON
Eaton Gallery, Princes Arcade, London
The Bridgeman Art Library

T

_____

_____

_____

_____

_____

_____

Give me a man with big hands, big feet, and no brains and I will make a golfer out of him.
WALTER HAGEN (1892-1969)

U

_____

_____

_____

_____

_____

_____

*The sport isn't like any other where a player can
take out all that is eating him on an opponent.
In golf, it's strictly you against your clubs.*
BOB ROSBURG

TOURNAMENT GOLFER HITTING BALL
BONNOT
The Image Bank

V

_____

_____

_____

_____

_____

_____

What other people may find in poetry or art
museums, I find in the flight of a good drive.
ARNOLD PALMER, B.1929

V

GOLFERS ON TROPICAL GOLF COURSE
MIKE VAUGHAN
The Image Bank

W

_____

_____

_____

_____

_____

_____

The pleasure of the long drive or second shot to
the green gives as fine an emotion as is possible
for any sinner to receive on this earth.
R.H. LYTTLETON

The average golfer doesn't play golf!
He attacks it.
JACKIE BURKE

GOLFER TEEING OFF – ACTION SHOT
BILL HALL
The Image Bank

Opposite: FRANCOIS DARDELET
The Image Bank

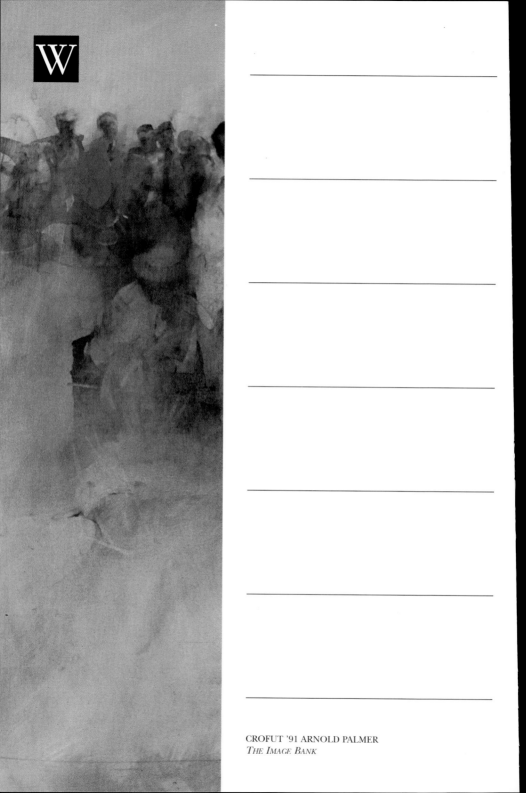

X Y Z

When I look on my life and try to decide out of what
I have got most actual pleasure, I have no doubt
that I have got more out of golf than anything else.
LORD BRABAZON